Brilliant Activities for

Creative Writing, Year 2

Activities for Developing Writing Composition Skills

Irene Yates

We hope you and your pupils enjoy using the ideas in this book. Brilliant Publications publishes many other books to help primary school teachers. To find out more details on all of our titles, including those listed below, please log onto our website: www.brilliantpublications.co.uk.

Other books in the Brilliant Activities for Creative Writing Series

Year 1	978-0-85747-463-6
Year 3	978-0-85747-465-0
Year 4	978-0-85747-466-7
Year 5	978-0-85747-467-4
Year 6	978-0-85747-468-1

Boost Creative Writing Series – Planning Sheets to Support Writers (Especially SEN Pupils)

Years 1–2	978-1-78317-058-6
Years 3–4	978-1-78317-059-3
Years 5–6	978-1-78317-060-9

Brilliant Activities for Reading Comprehension Series

Year 1	978-1-78317-070-8
Year 2	978-1-78317-071-5
Year 3	978-1-78317-072-2
Year 4	978-1-78317-073-9
Year 5	978-1-78317-074-6
Year 6	978-1-78317-075-3

Published by Brilliant Publications
Unit 10
Sparrow Hall Farm
Edlesborough
Dunstable
Bedfordshire
LU6 2ES, UK

Email: info@brilliantpublications.co.uk
Website: www.brilliantpublications.co.uk
Tel: 01525 222292

The name Brilliant Publications and the logo are registered trademarks.

Written by Irene Yates
Illustrated by Carol Jonas
Front cover illustration by Carol Jonas

© Text Irene Yates 2014
© Design Brilliant Publications 2014

Printed ISBN 978-0-85747-464-3
e-book ISBN 978-0-85747-471-1
First printed and published in the UK in 2014

The right of Irene Yates to be identified as the author of this work has been asserted by herself in accordance with the Copyright, Designs and Patents Act 1988.

Pages 6–47 may be photocopied by individual teachers acting on behalf of the purchasing institution for classroom use only, without permission from the publisher or declaration to the Publishers Licensing Society. The materials may not be reproduced in any other form or for any other purpose without the prior permission of the publisher.

Contents

- Introduction 4
- Links to the curriculum 5
- Choose a pet 6
- Autumn apples 7
- My toys 8
- Oh dear! 9
- My monster friend 10
- Happy day! 11
- Bad day 12
- Amazing day 13
- Falling asleep 14
- Teeth 15
- Cleaning teeth 16
- What do you think? 17
- What are they talking about? 18
- Way to go 19
- In the playground 20
- What makes a friend? 21
- Falling out 22
- Plan a story 23
- Lots of words 24
- Story-writing planner 25
- Make up a character 26
- This is my character 27
- Beginning a story 28
- Making sentences 29
- Visiting 30
- Who is this? 31
- Safety first 32
- Get fit! 33
- New playground 34
- Past, present and future 35
- Surprise! Surprise! 36
- Project on the Moon 37
- Seasons 38
- What does Robot do? 39
- My brother 40
- Make a list 41
- Last year 42
- Snail's pace 43
- Plan a story 44
- My writing 45
- Writing quiz 46
- Checklist for my writing 47

Introduction

The Brilliant Activities for Creative Writing series is designed to stimulate developing writers to access the National Curriculum Programmes of Study for writing composition.

Each book contains practice activities to assist pupils in understanding, revising and consolidating their skills in writing. The activities are structured to help each pupil to understand how to:

- write for a widening range of purposes and audiences
- organize ideas into coherent and grammatically correct sentences
- improve, and make progress in, their own writing
- increase their accuracy in the use of punctuation
- develop their knowledge and confidence in spelling
- use and enlarge their writing vocabulary
- write in different ways for different genres and types of text
- develop their own way with words

The sheets are structured but flexible so that they can be used alone or as follow-ons. The ideas on the sheets can all be used as a basis for more lessons for reinforcement purposes. Each book aims to offer:

- a range of familiar text forms
- a range of appropriate contexts
- opportunities to experiment with words drawn from language experience, literature and media
- opportunities to select vocabulary according to demands of activity
- use of proof-reading, checking and editing, sharing with peers
- encouragement to pupils to reflect upon their understanding of the writing process

Each activity is fully explained and the teacher tip boxes give hints and suggestions for making the most of them or for follow-up activities. No additional resources are necessary, other than writing implements and extra paper for more extended writing where it is appropriate. Children should be encouraged to talk about what they are going to write, prior to writing, with a partner, in groups or as a class. Discussing what they want to write, prior to doing so, will help them to structure their thoughts and ideas. Through careful questioning, adults can help children to develop their vocabulary and understanding of how language works.

Obviously, all of the activities would work well if the children are able to word process on a computer at some times – this would be an added bonus.

It is hoped that this series of books will encourage pupils to use their writing to reflect upon and monitor their own learning, to encourage them to read as writers and to write as readers and, more than anything else, to learn to write with joy.

Links to the curriculum

The sheets in **Brilliant Activities for Creative Writing** will help Year 2 pupils to develop their composition skills, as set out in the National Curriculum for England (2014).

Composition
The sheets in **Brilliant Activities for Creative Writing** provide opportunities for pupils to write a range of different types of writing, from narratives and instructional writing to information reports and poetry. They will not only learn how to write for different purposes, they will also develop stamina for writing.

The sheets are designed to encourage children to talk about what they are going to write prior to doing so. Many of the sheets have ideas and vocabulary that will act as prompts to stimulate pupils to discuss, prior to writing, what they want to say and how best to say it.

Pupils should be encouraged to re-read their work and make simple additions, revisions and corrections. Reading their writing aloud, to a teacher or other pupils, is a particularly valuable way of helping pupils to notice where and how their writing could be improved. In addition to checking for errors in spelling, grammar and punctuation, they should also be encouraged to check consistency of verb tenses.

Reading their writing aloud helps children to see that their writing is valued. The poetry sheets are particularly good for this.

Vocabulary, grammar and punctuation
Many of the sheets can be used to reinforce children's understanding of grammar and punctuation, but this is not the primary purpose of the sheets. Many sheets contain Word boxes to encourage children to extend their range of vocabulary and prompt them to use new words in their writing.

The following sheets deal with particular grammar and punctuation points:
- Autumn apples and Make a list (pages 7 and 41) encourage the use of conjunctions.
- Oh dear! (page 9) deals with exclamation marks.
- Falling out (page 22) focuses on verb endings.
- Making sentences (page 29) draws pupils' attention to the punctuation needed for sentences.
- Surprise! Surprise! (page 36) provides useful reinforcement on using apostrophes for contractions.
- Seasons (page 38) helps children to think about writing in paragraphs.
- What does Robot do? (page 39) focuses children's attention on verb tenses.

Choose a pet

Which one would you choose?

Why would you choose it?

Where would you keep it?

How would you feed it?

What if it escapes?

- -

- -

- -

Don't forget:
Use full stops and capital letters.

Encourage talk to plan. Show how to write down key words. Sequence ideas before beginning the writing.

Autumn apples

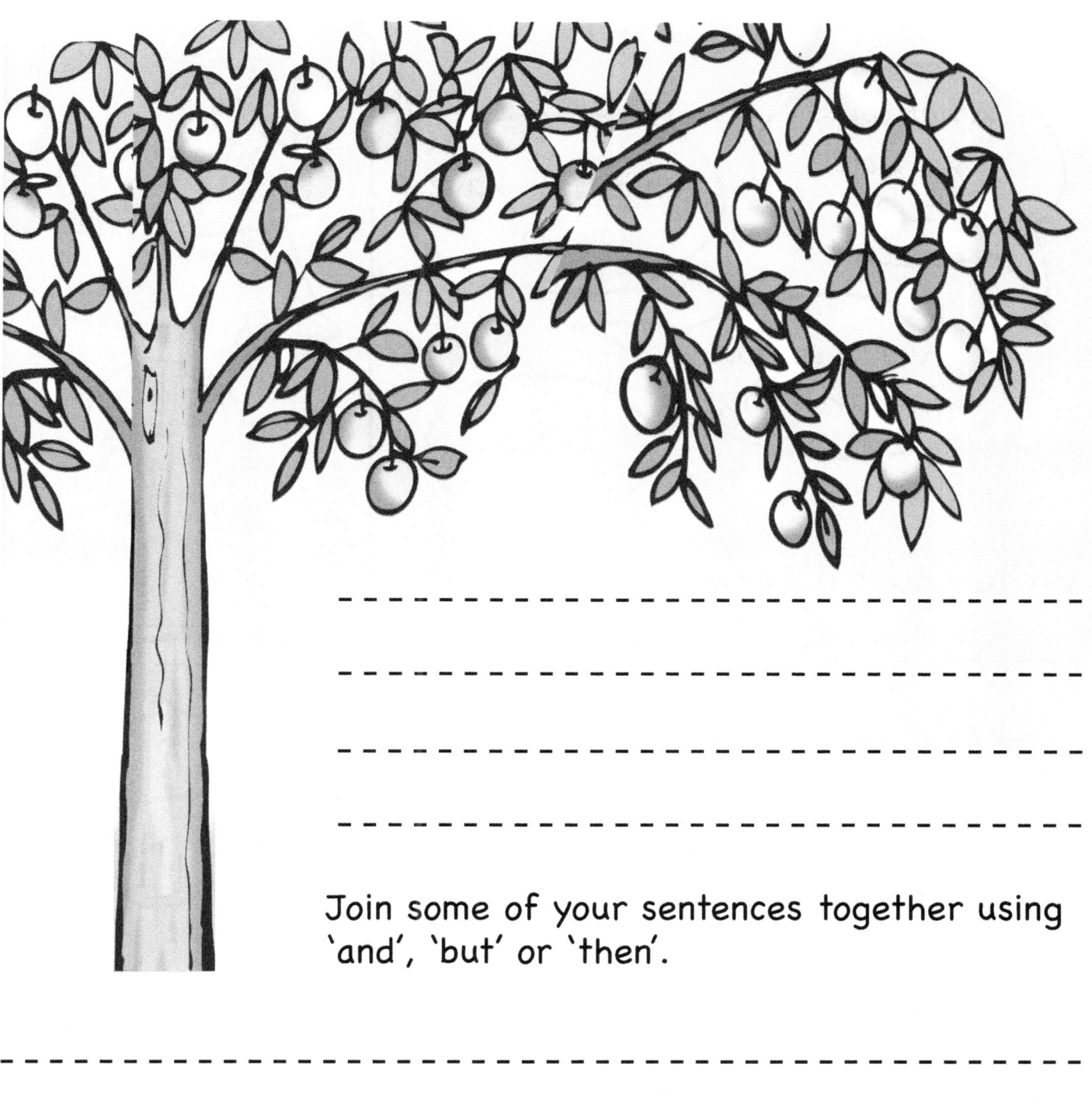

Join some of your sentences together using 'and', 'but' or 'then'.

Discuss aloud, drawing on real events or ideas from fiction to help composition. Plan. Sequence.

My toys

What toys can you see?

What toys have you got?

Which is your favourite toy?

Why?

Write about it here:

Word box

toys	play	help
like	best	share
	together	

Lots of talk. Talk to plan. Make notes of key words. Write and read.

Oh dear!

- What is happening in the picture?
- Then what is going to happen?
- What's going to happen next?
- How might it all end?

Remember:
Use exclamation marks where the story is exciting!

Talk through the pictures and possibilities. Plan sentences verbally. Sequence sentences. Check writing.

My monster friend

Draw a picture of a monster.

My monster is: _____

Write what you said to each other when you met. Use speech bubbles.

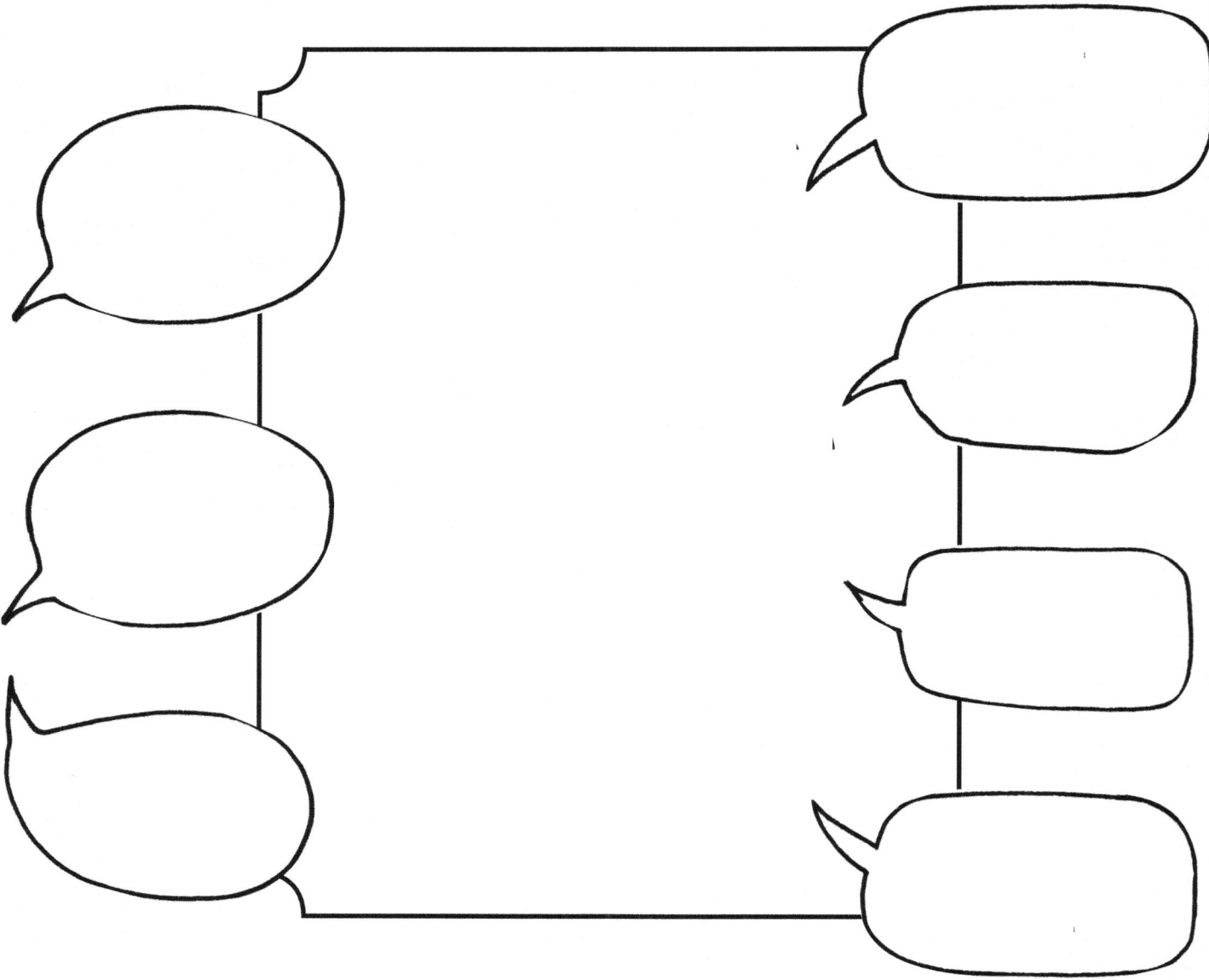

Talk about the monster character. It needs a name and a description. How does is move? How does it communicate? Work on strong, descriptive verbs and creating character.

Happy day!

Pick a happy person and write their story.

Lots of talk about the characters. Help choose and create a character and story by asking open questions and developing ideas. Plan, sequence and feed vocabulary.

Brilliant Activities for Creative Writing, Year 2
© Irene Yates and Brilliant Publications

Bad day

Let's choose someone to cheer up!

Lots of talk. Choose a character and create a story. Ask open questions and help to develop ideas. Write down key words and new vocabulary before composing.

Amazing day

The most amazing thing that happened was ...

Word box

enormous
fabulous
huge
beautiful

Try this:
Use an exclamation mark somewhere in your story.

Lots of talk about 'amazing' events, real or imaginary. Do short improvisation on amazement. Discuss physical and mental responses. Practise sentences before writing.

Falling asleep

What's Ryan's grandad going to talk about? What do you think happens next?

Where does the story happen?

When does the story happen?

Who does the story happen to?

How does the story end?

Lots of talk about what the 'talk' could have been about, why the grandad fell asleep, what happened next. Help children to sequence a narrative and form sentences before writing.

Teeth

It started with just a little wobble and then ...

Lots of talk about personal experience of tooth-wobble, spaces in teeth, the tooth fairy, etc. Focus on first person writing in the past tense.

Cleaning teeth

How to clean your teeth properly.

What you need:

What you do:

The best way to look after your teeth is to:

Talk about and name what can be seen. Show how to make a list using bullet points. Check everything is on the list. Talk and then write.

What do you think?

smart, trendy, baggy, scruffy, posh, unusual, favourite, fashionable, pretty, clean, striped

Draw and write about your own favourites. Try to use some of the adjectives.

Lots of discussion. You are looking for the suggestion of 'clothes'. Verbalize before writing. Read and share.

What are they talking about?

Draw and write about your favourite. Try to use some of the nouns.

Lots of discussion. You are looking for the suggestion of 'food'. Verbalize before writing. Read and share.

Way to go

Can you find a noun for every kind of transport shown? The one below has come to take you to school.

Write the story.

Can you use any of the nouns?

Lots of talk about transport. Discussion about how different it would be to go to school in a horse-drawn carriage before writing.

Brilliant Activities for Creative Writing, Year 2
© Irene Yates and Brilliant Publications

In the playground

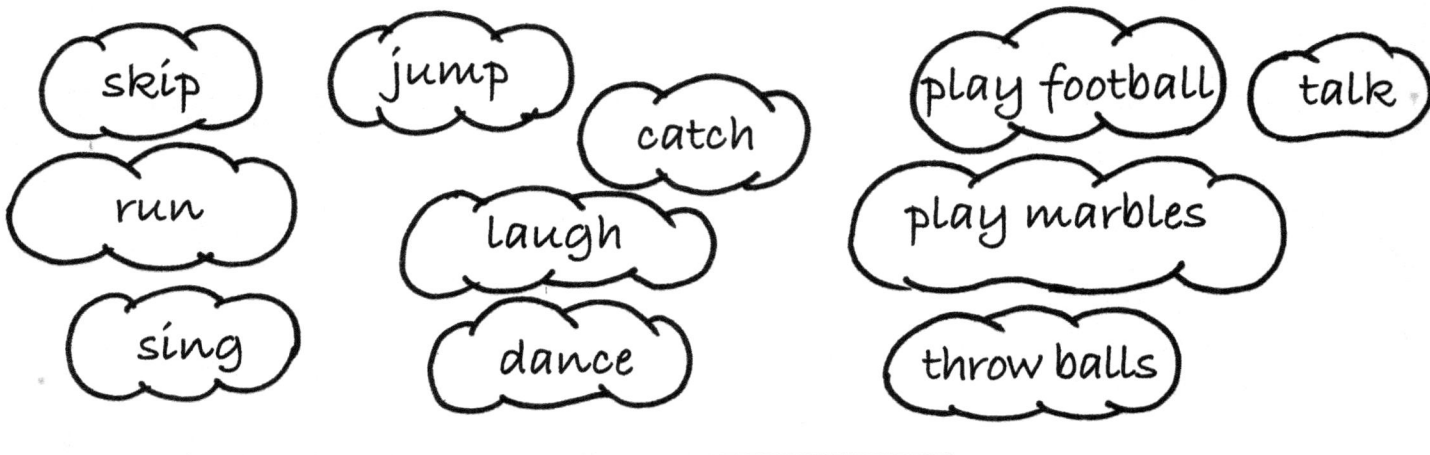

These children are talking about things they do in the playground at break-time. Draw and write about your favourite. Try to use some of the verbs.

Lots of talk about the picture. Work out the whole sentence.

What makes a friend?

- being kind
- doing things together
- liking the same things
- sticking up for each other
- looking after one another
- sharing

Make some rules for how to be a good friend.

Try to learn a new word and how to spell it.

Lots of talk about friendship. Plan and say aloud the rules the children should use before they write them down.

Falling out

- arguing
- stamping your feet
- losing your temper
- falling out
- upsetting
- shouting
- crying
- being cross

What happens when you have a falling out with your friends?

It's not nice.

Write a story about falling out.

Try to learn a new word and how to spell it.

Lots of discussion about personal experience. Show how the verb endings change to 'ing'.

Plan a story

Who will be in your story?	Where will your story take place?

What will happen in your story?	How will it end?

When you have made notes in these boxes, tell your story to someone.

Lots of talk about how to plan a story and how a story works. Give children a chance to make notes and/or draw and then to tell their story verbally.

Lots of words

Words about my character (Who)	Words about the place (Where)
Words about events (What)	Words about endings (How)

Choose and write some words to help you write your story.

Here are a few words to give you ideas.
Who: dinosaur, Mum, boy, girl, princess, wizard.
Where: castle, school, home, beach, playground, an island, in space.
What: adventure, mystery, crash, fight, game, being lost, being in trouble.
How: friends, found, never, best, happy, peace, sorted

Lots of verbalization about characters, settings, events and endings. Demonstrate choices in boxes and show how these can be used to write narrative.

Story-writing planner

Title: _____

Who? _____

When? _____

Where? _____

What goes wrong? _____

Then what happens? _____

How is it all solved? _____

Help children to plan, make notes and when they are ready, write their story.

Make up a character

Who is your character?

What does he/she look like?

Where does he/she live?

What is he/she like?

The people, animals or aliens in stories are called 'characters'. When you write a story you have to think carefully about them. You start by making notes about them, like these:

Characters also might be:
robots
or
monsters
or
super heros
or
toys

Name: _____

What the character looks like:

_____

_____

_____

What sort of being the character is:

_____

Talk about lots of characters the children have already met in stories, films, programmes and games. Analyze some of these characters together in this way before the children make up their own.

This is my character

There was once a

_ _ _ _ _ _ _ _ _ _ _ _ _ _ _ _ _ _ _ _

Whose name was

_ _ _ _ _ _ _ _ _ _ _ _ _ _ _ _ _ _ _ _

This is how _ _ _ _ _ _ _ _ _ _ _ _

looked _ _ _ _ _ _ _ _ _ _ _ _ _ _

had _ _ _ _ _ _ _ _ _ _ _ _ _ _ _ _ _ _

and _ _ _ _ _ _ _ _ _ _ _ _ _ _ _ _ _ _

and _ _ _ _ _ _ _ _ _ _ _ _ _ _ _ _ _ .

_ _ _ _ _ _ _ _ _ _ _ was

always _ _ _ _ _ _ _ _ _ _ _

and _ .

Then one day _

_ _

These words might help you:
girl, boy, alien, fish, monster, he, she, it, kind, generous, friendly, bad, naughty, angry, lazy, shy

Discuss, explore and develop ideas for character creation, before children complete the page.

Beginning a story

The beginning of a story always tells you where and when it is happening. This is called 'the setting'.

Write down places a story could happen, the 'Where'.

_____

_____

_____

_____

Write down times a story could happen, the 'When'.

_____

_____

_____

These words might help you:
Long, long ago; In the future; Yesterday; Last week; When you were born; In the past; Tomorrow; In the year 3020

Talk about stories, films, programmes that the children know and extract ideas about the settings. Make notes about ones that really capture the children's interest for future projects.

Making sentences

Every sentence starts with a capital letter and ends with a punctuation mark.

    .   full stop
    ?   question mark
    !   exclamation mark

Every sentence needs to make sense.

Sentence	*Not a sentence*
The baby can crawl.	The baby crawl.
Grandad is asleep.	Grandad asleep.
It is raining.	It rain.

Write some sentences about what is happening, right now, where you are.

_____

_____

_____

_____

_____

Check:
Full stops, capital letters. Does it make sense?

Lots of talk and demonstration about these concepts. The children should be able to check in available books and resources looking for sentence punctuation.

Visiting

Write a story about a visit. Before you write the story, make notes about when, where and who did the visiting.

When	Where	Who
-------------	-------------	-------------
-------------	-------------	-------------
-------------	-------------	-------------
-------------	-------------	-------------
-------------	-------------	-------------

Use your notes to write the story.

Recap on setting and character. Plunder, explore and develop ideas for the 'visiting' situation. Write key words on the board.

Who is this?

Draw and write notes about one character in each of these circles.

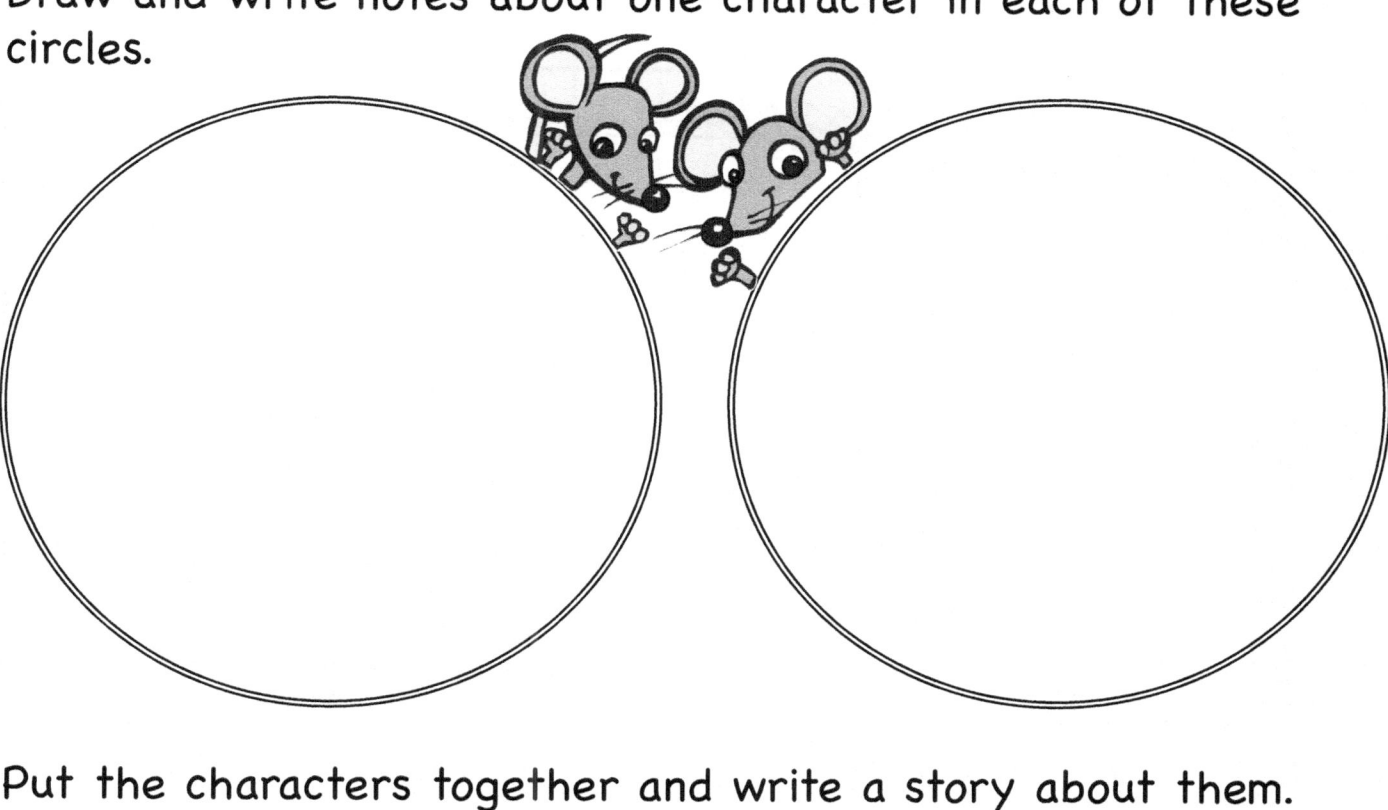

Put the characters together and write a story about them.

_____

_____

_____

_____

_____

Remember:
The characters do not have to be humans. They might be animals, aliens, dinosaurs, cars – or anything or anyone you wish, as long as they can go in a story.

Recap 'character' discussion. Lots of talk and exploration of ideas to aid creativity.

Safety first

Design a *Safety First* poster to put into your school.

On your poster:
- Explain the dangers to children
- Explain to parents what they should do
- Explain how healthy it is to walk to school
- Explain how everyone can make coming to school and leaving school much better.

Make up a slogan, like this:

Be safe! Be healthy!

Stress the purpose of the writing. Talk through safety issues and through poster design. Verbalize sentences before writing. Display posters. Ask for responses.

Get fit!

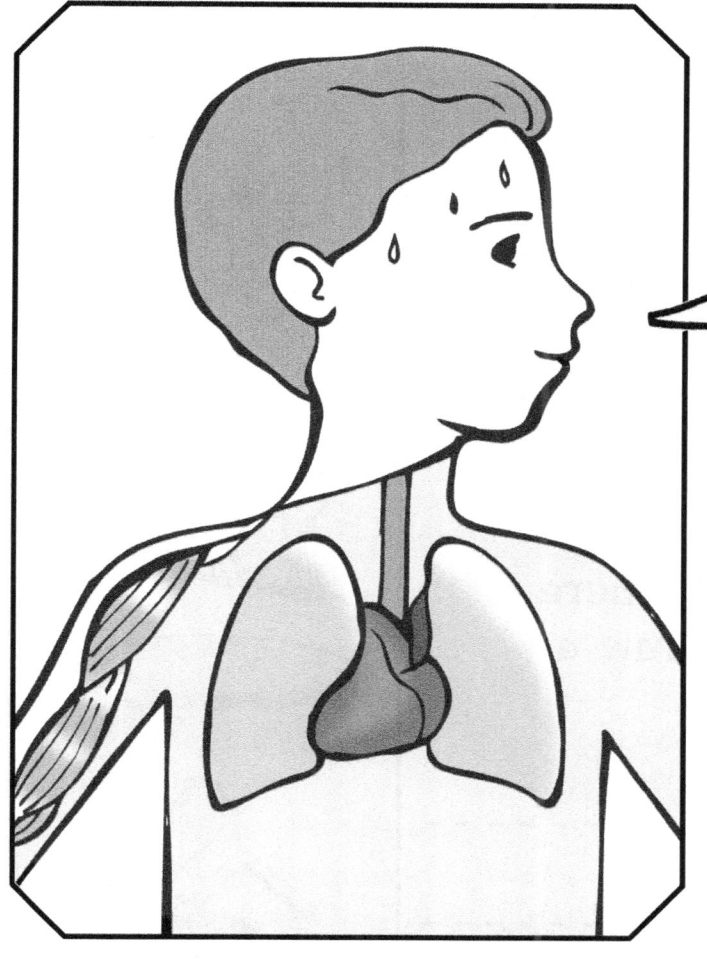

What happens to my body when I exercise?

Exercise is good for us. It makes our muscles strong and keeps us fit and healthy. How many different kinds of exercise can you do?

Think about your:
Heart?
Muscles?
Body temperature?
Energy?

Make a list, using bullet points.
I can:

◆ _____

◆ _____

◆ _____

◆ _____

Compare your list with the rest of your group.

Stress the purpose of the writing. Focus on writing for information, keeping the sentences clear and concise. Plan and verbalize before writing.

New playground

I think the new playground should have lots of activities to help keep us healthy.

Write down your ideas for designing a new playground.

What would you like it to have? Where would the different things be? Draw a diagram to help you.

Use some of these words		
or	and	but
when	under	beside
over	next to	opposite

Show how to jot down ideas and key words. Share and evaluate verbally. Proof read and edit.

Past, present and future

Above
"This is what the traffic was like in the past."

Right
"This is what the traffic is like now."

Write some information about travelling in the past, the present and the future. Make sure you get the tense of the verbs right.

Draw what you think our transport will be like in the future.

" … and in the future it will be … ."

Talk about verb tenses. Provide lots of demonstration. Talk about the illustrations and garner ideas for illustrations of future travel.

Surprise! Surprise!

Ayesha's waiting for the postman.

It's her birthday!

What's in the parcel?

Write the story.

_____

_____

_____

_____

_____

_____

_____

Make these smaller, using apostrophes:
She is
It is   _____
There is   _____
They are _____
What is   _____
Ayesha is _____
Are not   _____
Can not   _____

Use them in your story.

Words to help
huge   present   parcel
curious ribbon   string

Discuss using apostrophes for contractions. Read the stories aloud and share. Encourage responses.

Project on the Moon

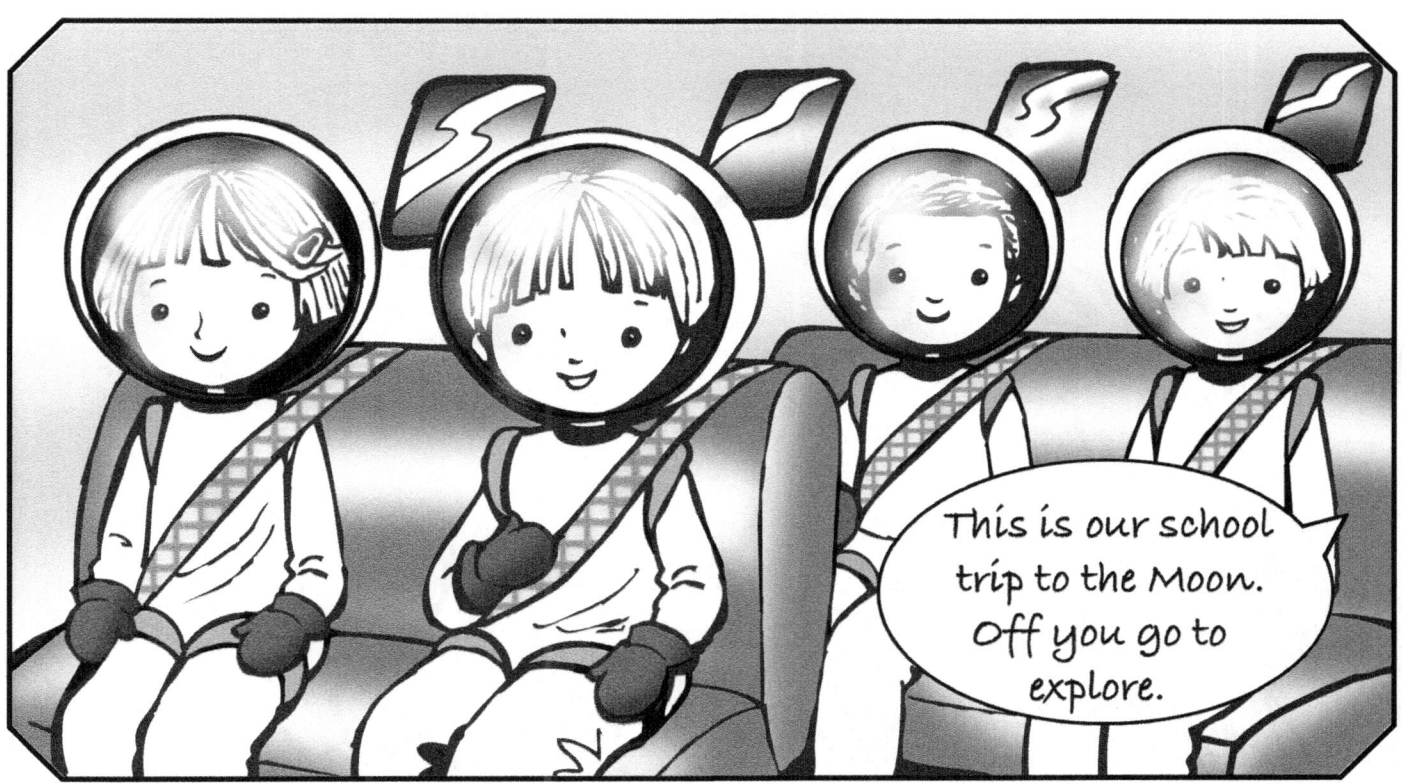

Write a blog about your Moon trip to tell everyone what a great time you're having.

- How did you travel?
- What does the Moon look/smell/feel/taste like?
- Who lives there?
- How is it different from Earth?
- What is 'time' like?

Check your sentences, punctuation and verb tenses before you send your blog.

> **Words to help**   astronaut, moon, sun, moonbeam, crater, sandy, rocky, spaceship, galaxy, stars, Earth, moon people, moon school, lessons, telescope, bounce, spacesuit

Lots of talk to stimulate, explore and develop ideas. Encourage children to use their imagination.

Seasons

Write a calendar-story using proper sentences about things that happen in the seasons. Winter is started to show you how.

In the winter it's freezing on the way to school. We all wear coats and hats and gloves and scarves to keep warm.

Try to use the words: though, unless, because.

Words to help					
cold	crisp	fresh	snow	rain	storm
foggy	winter	autumn	spring	summer	dull
grey	blue,	breeze	breezy	wet	drizzle

Go through the seasons and what happens during them. Stress the use of paragraphs for each change of idea.

What does Robot do?

Write an advertisement for the robot you have invented.

Make sure the tense of verbs stays the same all the way through. You could make your advertisement into a poem, if you wanted to.

Words to help					
bump	eat	fall	play	sing	walk
mix	ride	go	ask	to	do
wish					

Lots of discussion about robots and verbs and tense agreement. Stress the persuasive idea of an advertisement.

My brother

Read the start of this poem:

My brother had a party
They wouldn't let me play,

_____

_____

_____

_____

Make up some more words for this poem and write them above. Lines 4 and 6 need to rhyme with line 2. Clap the pattern out to help you. Write more verses.

_____

_____

_____

_____

_____

Words to help (all these words rhyme)						
day	lay	play	sleigh	may	pay	grey
spray	tray	stay	say	stray	they	way

Lots of talk to generate ideas. Discuss alliteration and reward use of it. Read, share and comment after writing.

Make a List

Use the alphabet to write a list poem, like this:

I walk to school each morning,
There's such a lot to see,
I see
Acorns and
Aeroplanes and
Babies and
Buggies and...

You could use commas instead of the words 'and' until you get to the last but one item. Try both ways to find out which sounds the best when you recite it, eg I see acorns, aeroplanes, babies, buggies...

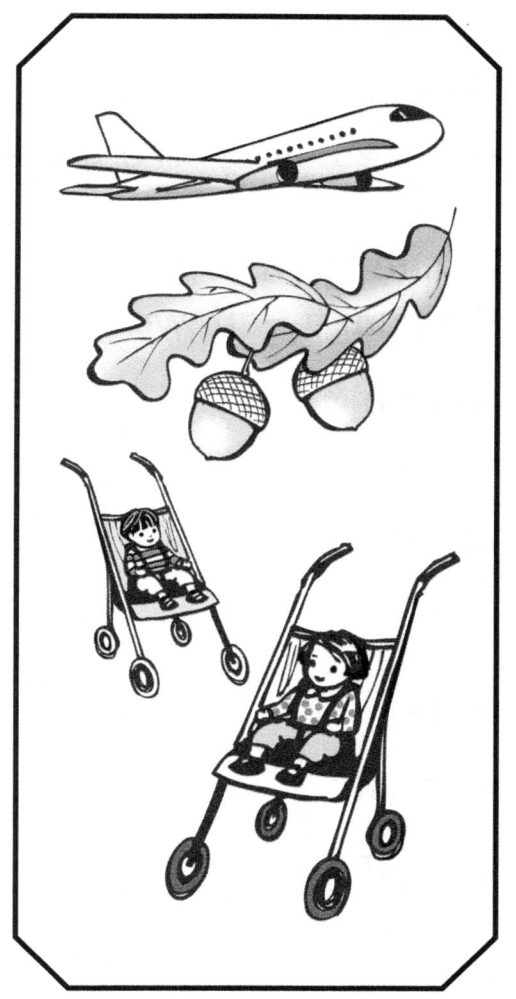

Recap the alphabet and the conjunction 'and'. Lots of talk to share fun ideas. Read, share and comment after writing.

Last year

Write a poem about things that happened last year, using repeating sounds. January and February are done to show you how.

January was jolly cold. Brrrrrr, Brrrrrr.
February – it was freezing. Shiver, shiver.

March

April

May

June

July

August

September

October

November

December

Words to help:

cold	crisp	fresh	snow	rain	storm
foggy	sunny	frosty	winter	autumn	spring
summer	dull	grey	blue	breeze	breezy
wet	drizzle				

Recap the months of the year and what they bring to the seasons. Jot down key words and phrases. Stress spelling and unusual ideas.

Snail's pace

This is how you write an acrostic poem:

Slow as slow
Never hurrying
Anywhere
In case he
Loses his shell.

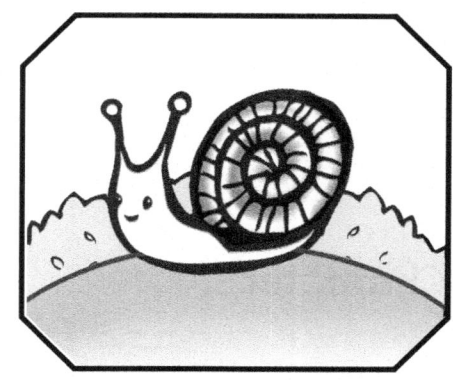

Start with the word written downwards. Use the first letter to start the first word of the line.

S _____
Q _____
U _____
I _____
R _____
R _____
E _____
L _____

R _____
O _____
B _____
I _____
N _____

Extra ideas:
butterfly   seagull   crab   fish   tortoise

Demonstrate acrostic poems on the board. Stress the use of good, strong adjectives. Share aloud and comment.

Plan a story

Title: --

Character: --

Setting: --

Beginning: --

Middle: --

Ending: --

My writing

Write three things you like about writing.

1. _____

2. _____

3. _____

Write three things you don't like about writing.

1. _____

2. _____

3. _____

What kind of writing do you like best?

1. _____

2. _____

3. _____

Talk first, but you want the children's own perceptions of their writing to shine through.

Writing quiz

Do you know what this is and when to u se it?
Put a ✔ in the box.

	Yes	Not sure	No
a sentence	☐	☐	☐
a capital letter	☐	☐	☐
a full stop	☐	☐	☐
fiction	☐	☐	☐
story	☐	☐	☐
diagram	☐	☐	☐
poem	☐	☐	☐
rhyme	☐	☐	☐
non-fiction	☐	☐	☐
noun	☐	☐	☐
adjective	☐	☐	☐
instruction	☐	☐	☐
letter	☐	☐	☐
word	☐	☐	☐

Do this as a class quiz. Children to tick yes, not sure or no boxes but expect them to be able to describe meaning if they tick 'yes'.

This page may be photocopied for use by the purchasing institution only.

Checklist for my writing

✓   I've written a brilliant story!

☐   Have I got a beginning, middle and end?
Notes:

☐   Have I got a good character?
Notes:

☐   Have I written proper sentences that make sense?
Notes:

☐   Have my sentences got capital letters and full stops?
Notes:

☐   Have I used the right verbs?
Notes:

☐   Have I always used the right tense?
Notes:

☐   Have I made sure I've used the same pronoun all the way through and haven't changed, for instance, from 'he' to 'I'?
Notes:

☐   Have I checked my spelling?
Notes:

Use this sheet for every piece of writing to help you to edit. Put your mistakes right on your second draft.

Get children used to thinking these things through when they finish writing.

Brilliant Activities for Creative Writing, Year 2
© Irene Yates and Brilliant Publications

Lightning Source UK Ltd.
Milton Keynes UK
UKOW05f2123250816

281475UK00004B/72/P